WRITER'S
TOOLBOX

Share a Scare
Writing Your Own Scary Story

by Nancy Loewen   illustrated by Christopher Lyles

Picture Window Books
Minneapolis, Minnesota

Editor: Jill Kalz
Designer: Nathan Gassman
Page Production: Melissa Kes
Editorial Director: Nick Healy
Creative Director: Joe Ewest
The illustrations in this book were created
with acrylic and collage on illustration board.

Picture Window Books
1710 Roe Crest Drive
P.O. Box 669
North Mankato, MN 56003-0669
877-845-8392
www.capstonepub.com

Library of Congress Cataloging-in-Publication Data
Loewen, Nancy, 1964–
Share a scare : writing your own scary story /
by Nancy Loewen ; illustrated by Christopher Lyles.
p. cm. — (Writer's toolbox)
Includes webliography and index.
ISBN 978-1-4048-5517-5 (library binding)
ISBN 978-1-4048-5700-1 (paperback)
1. Horror tales—Authorship—Juvenile literature.
I. Lyles, Christopher, 1977- ill. II. Title.
PN3377.5.H67L64 2009
808.83'872—dc22   2009003299

Printed in the United States of America in North Mankato, Minnesota.
062013   007364R

Special thanks to our adviser, Terry Flaherty, Ph.D., Professor of
English, Minnesota State University, Mankato, for his expertise.

Goosebumps and gasps. Shivers and quivers. Shudders and trembles and shakes.

Is it possible that these experiences could be *fun*?

Sure—if you're reading a scary story!

Scary stories invite us into the dark, spooky side of our imaginations. They challenge us every step of the way. At the end, we might still be scared, but we have a feeling of victory, too. Maybe that's why so many people love scary stories!

In this book, you'll learn how to write your own scary story. Start by reading our example, "The Scary-Go-Round," straight through. Then go back to page 5 and learn about the tools you can use to give your readers chills and thrills.

"Let's take that trail," Shane said.

"Let's not," argued Lila.

Lila and Shane had walked their dog at the park dozens of times. But they'd never noticed the side trail. It was a line of trampled-down grass, going up a small hill.

"I think we should go home," Lila said.
"The sun is setting. It'll be dark soon."

Shane ignored her and headed up the trail.

Lila sighed. "Come on, Beans," she said to their dog.

~ Tool 1 ~

One of the first things a reader learns in a good scary story is the **SETTING.** When does the story take place? Where does it happen? Scary stories often take place in dark locations. In this story, the setting is a park at sunset.

~ Tool 2 ~

Scary stories introduce readers to at least one of the main **CHARACTERS** right away. Characters are the people or creatures in the story. The main characters are the ones who appear most often. Here we meet Shane, Lila, and their dog, Beans.

~ Tool 3 ~

SENSORY DETAILS help readers see, hear, smell, taste, and touch what's going on in the story. Here we *see* the splintered wood of the teeter-totter. We *see* the merry-go-round covered in vines and spider webs. We *hear* the rusty chains of the old swing set.

~ Tool 4 ~

FORESHADOWING is often used in scary stories. Foreshadowing gives readers hints about what might happen later in the story. Lila thinks the old playground is creepy. She's uneasy. And because she's worried, so are we.

They stopped at the top of the hill. Below them, in a clearing surrounded by trees, was an old playground.

"Cool!" Shane exclaimed.

"Creepy," Lila muttered.

They hiked down the hill until they reached a swing set made of rotting wood. The rusty chains creaked in the breeze. A splintery teeter-totter stood in a cluster of thorny bushes. Next to it was a merry-go-round covered in vines and spider webs.

"Let's go back," Lila said with a shiver.

"Oh, all right," Shane said. "I'll come back tomorrow—by myself."

~ Tool 5 ~

Together, all the events that make up a story are called the **PLOT**.

Something moved in the woods. Beans growled.

"What was *that*?" Lila asked.

"Oh, probably a giant chicken, or a two-headed fox, or—"

Shane stopped short. An old woman, her head wrapped in black, was hobbling toward them. Her skin was so wrinkly it seemed to be slipping off her face.

"Play with me?" she begged. "Play with me?"

~ Tool 6 ~

The plots of scary stories are full of **SURPRISES.** Strange, unexpected things happen. Shane and Lila (and Beans) are startled to see an old woman at the playground. Who is she? What is she doing there?

"Um, hi," Shane said nervously as Lila clutched his arm. This was too weird. What would an old lady be doing out here at sunset?

The woman seemed to read his mind. "I come here by myself all the time," she said. "I live just over there, on Willow Road."

Shane and Lila glanced at each other. There was no Willow Road. Not anymore. No one lived inside the park. Their own house was the closest one to the entrance.

~ Tool 7 ~

The mystery of the old woman deepens. Shane and Lila don't know what to think. Neither do we! Is the old woman simply lost and confused? Or is there something spooky going on? It's too soon to say. But the **SUSPENSE** continues to build.

"Play with me?" the old woman said again. There was something odd about her eyes. Looking into them was like looking through dirty windows and seeing two small red flames. But maybe that was just the sunset reflecting in her eyes.

~ Tool 8 ~

Sometimes, writers use words to create a picture in readers' minds. This is called **IMAGERY**. The words might compare one thing to another. Here, the woman's eyes are likened to dirty windows with small flames glowing behind them. What if they had been compared to red licorice? Would you feel differently about her?

Beans tugged hard at his leash, trying to pull the kids back toward the trail.

"Don't go! Play with me!" The woman stamped her foot weakly.
"Play with me!"

Lila and Shane whispered to each other, then turned back toward the woman. "Don't be upset. I'll play with you," Lila said in a polite but trembling voice. "What do you want to do?"

~ Tool 9 ~

DIALOGUE is what characters say to each other. Dialogue gives information and helps move the story along. Readers "hear" the characters talk. They feel like the story is happening right in front of them.

The woman pressed her hands together in delight. "The merry-go-round is my favorite. You go first!"

"It's not going to work," Shane whispered to Lila. "Obviously. It hasn't been used in years. And how is she going to be able to push you?"

The woman heard him. "Oh, I'm a real good pusher!"

Lila shrugged helplessly at Shane. She climbed onto the merry-go-round, staying well away from the spider webs.

"Hold on tight!" the woman ordered.

Lila carefully placed her hands on a rotting wooden handle. The old woman leaned forward.

The merry-go-round creaked ... roots tore out of the ground ... and then it slowly began to spin. The old woman let go, but the merry-go-round kept moving. It picked up speed.

"Lila!" Shane shouted. This was too strange. They needed to get out of here. "Let's go home. NOW!"

But the merry-go-round whirred faster and faster. The old woman clapped her hands. Her eyes glowed brighter—the red flames grew bigger—

"**Shane!**" Lila cried. She crouched down and tried to jump off the merry-go-round. But it was going too fast. Around and around—

~ Tool 10 ~

Scary stories work best if the main characters **TAKE ACTION.** They can't just have things done *to* them. They need to fight back! Shane can't stop the merry-go-round. But that just makes the story more frightening.

20

Shane dropped Beans' leash
and ran to the merry-go-round.
He tried to put his foot on the edge
and grab the handle. But the spinning
merry-go-round threw him to the ground.

21

"**Stop this thing!**" Shane yelled at the old woman.

"**You're scaring my sister!**"

The woman smiled, her eyes brighter than ever. She held up a bony hand and the merry-go-round began to slow down. Slower ... and slower ... and slower.

~ Tool 11 ~

In all types of stories, **PUNCTUATION** can make a scene come alive. Exclamation points show strong feelings, such as anger or fear. Ellipses (the three dots after the word *slower*) create a pause.

The ellipses here make us feel the merry-go-round slowing down. On page 18, the dashes create a feeling of speed as the merry-go-round goes faster.

When the merry-go-round stopped, Lila stepped off.

"Are you all right?" Shane asked.

"Oh yes," Lila replied. "That was fun! Now it's your turn!"

She brushed the hair out of her eyes and looked straight at Shane.

He gasped.

~ Tool 12 ~

The **CLIMAX** is often the scariest part of a scary story. Everything that happened earlier in the story has led us to this moment.

Lila's eyes burned into his like a red flame.

~ Tool 13 ~

In most kinds of stories, the **ENDING** should leave readers satisfied. All the questions in the story have been answered. But scary stories are different. A good scary story should leave readers with their hearts pounding!

She took the old woman's hand and together they stepped toward Shane.

"Play with us!" they begged.

"Play with us!"

Let's Review!

These are the **13 tools** you need to write great scary stories.

The **SETTING (1)** of a scary story helps set the mood. The **CHARACTERS (2)** are the people or creatures in the story. **SENSORY DETAILS (3)** appeal to our five senses and help readers connect to the story.

FORESHADOWING (4) provides clues about events that will happen. Together, the events in a story make up the **PLOT (5)**. Scary stories should include **SURPRISES (6)**. **SUSPENSE (7)** builds throughout the story and keeps the reader turning pages. **IMAGERY (8)** is language that lets readers create pictures in their minds. Characters speak to each other (and give information to the reader) through **DIALOGUE (9)**. They **TAKE ACTION (10)** to solve their problems. **PUNCTUATION (11)** such as ellipses, dashes, and exclamation points can speed up or slow down the story's events.

The **CLIMAX (12)** is the peak of the story's action and is likely to be the scariest moment. The reader shouldn't feel happy or calm with the **ENDING (13)** of a scary story—the reader should feel scared!

Getting Started Exercises

- Have you ever been lost at a store, or heard a strange noise outside your window, or thought something was following you in the woods? What details do you remember? Ask your friends and family to share their scary stories. Once you get a basic idea, let your imagination take over.

- Do you remember what you dressed up as last Halloween? How about the year before that—and the year before that? Imagine those characters all together, and put them in a scary setting. What might happen?

- Dreams can be very strange, and some of them are scary. What dreams do you remember? Could any of them be used in a story?

- Scary movies often have sequels. A sequel is a story that starts where the one before it ended. Pick out a favorite scary book or movie, and see if you can keep the plot going.

Writing Tips

 Think about your five senses: seeing, hearing, touching, smelling, and tasting. Pick details that connect to those senses. You'll send shivers down your readers' spines!

 Read your story out loud—to yourself at first, and then to your friends and family. Turn out the lights and read by flashlight, to put everyone in the right mood. Pay attention to how your story sounds. Are there places that move too slowly, or too fast? Do all of your details help create a scary feeling?

 Remember that there are lots of types of scary stories. Some have the traditional scary characters and settings—ghosts, haunted houses, and so on. Other scary stories are more like real life. What matters is that, in the end, the reader is spooked!

Glossary

character—a person, animal, or creature in a story

climax—a story's most exciting moment

delight—great enjoyment or pleasure

detail—one of many facts about a certain thing

dialogue—the words spoken between two or more characters; in writing, dialogue is set off with quotation marks

ending—the last of three main story parts; the finish

foreshadowing—giving hints about what might happen in the future

imagery—words used to create pictures in readers' minds

plot—what happens in a story

punctuation—marks used to make written language clear; examples include periods, commas, and question marks

sensory—having to do with the five senses: sight, smell, hearing, taste, and touch

setting—the time and place of a story

suspense—worry, unease

trampled—to be walked on many times, crushed

whir—to spin very fast

To Learn More

More Books to Read

Bollinger, Peter. *Algernon Graeves Is Scary Enough.* New York: Laura Geringer Books, 2005.

Hoberman, Mary Ann. *You Read to Me, I'll Read to You: Very Short Scary Tales to Read Together.* New York: Little, Brown and Co., 2007.

Powling, Chris, ed. *Supershorts: Seriously Spooky Stories.* New York: Kingfisher, 2007.

Internet Sites

FactHound offers a safe, fun way to find Internet sites related to this book. All of the sites on FactHound have been researched by our staff.

Here's what you do:
Visit *www.facthound.com*
FactHound will fetch the best sites for you!

Index

action, 20, 28
characters, 5, 14, 20, 28, 29, 30
climax, 24, 28
details, 6, 28, 29, 30
dialogue, 14, 28
ending, 26, 28
foreshadowing, 6, 28
imagery, 12, 28
plot, 8, 9, 28, 29
punctuation, 22, 28
senses, 6, 28, 30
setting, 5, 28, 29, 30
surprises, 9, 28
suspense, 11, 28

Look for all of the books in the Writer's Toolbox series:

It's All About You: Writing Your Own Journal
Just the Facts: Writing Your Own Research Report
Make Me Giggle: Writing Your Own Silly Story
Once Upon a Time: Writing Your Own Fairy Tale

Share a Scare: Writing Your Own Scary Story
Show Me a Story: Writing Your Own Picture Book
Sincerely Yours: Writing Your Own Letter
Words, Wit, and Wonder: Writing Your Own Poem